The Over-Soul

Mystical Insights into Universal Spirit & the Divine Within Each Person

A Modern Translation

Adapted for the Contemporary Reader

Ralph Waldo Emerson

Translated by Tim Zengerink

Table Of Contents

Preface
Message to the Reader

Rebuilding the Greatest Library in Human History

Thousands of years ago, the Library of Alexandria was the heart of global knowledge — a sanctuary where the wisdom of every known civilization was gathered and shared freely.

And then, it was lost.

Now, we're rebuilding it — and you are invited to join us.

At the Library of Alexandria, we've set out to make every book available to every person on Earth — not just in print, but in every language, every format, and for every reader.

Here's how we do it:

- **Deluxe Print Editions at True Printing Cost** - Order any book as a high-quality paperback, elegant hardcover, or stunning boxset — and only pay what it costs to print. No markups. No middlemen.
- **Unlimited Access to the Greatest Works** - Enjoy thousands of timeless classics — from Plato to Shakespeare to Tolstoy — in beautiful, modern eBook and audiobook editions. Read and listen without limits — for every reader, everywhere.
- **Modern Translations for Every Language & Dialect** - We're reimagining the classics in clear, accessible language — and translating them into every dialect imaginable. Everyone deserves to understand humanity's greatest ideas.

When you visit **LibraryofAlexandria.com**, you're not just accessing books — you're joining a global movement to restore, preserve, and share the wisdom of civilization.

Join us today at LibraryofAlexandria.com

Together, we'll ensure the light of human wisdom never fades again.

With gratitude,

The Modern Library of Alexandria Team

Visit:
www.libraryofalexandria.com
Or scan the code below:

Introduction

Emerson's Vision of Spiritual Unity

Ralph Waldo Emerson's essay *The Over-Soul*, first published in 1841 in the second series of his collected Essays, stands as one of the most profound and mystical articulations of his transcendentalist philosophy. In its pages, Emerson attempts to capture in language what is, by nature, ineffable: the presence of a divine spirit that unites all beings, transcends individuality, and manifests through intuition, truth, beauty, and moral goodness. More than a theological speculation or philosophical treatise, *The Over-Soul* is a spiritual meditation—a lyrical unfolding of Emerson's inner revelations and a bold reaffirmation of the unity of existence.

In an age increasingly defined by materialism, sectarianism, and industrial expansion, Emerson sought to reawaken the spiritual consciousness of his readers. While many in his Unitarian tradition leaned toward rational religion and historical Christianity, Emerson turned inward, seeking a more direct, intuitive, and universal experience of the divine. He believed that true spirituality was not mediated through ritual, clergy, or doctrine but discovered in the quiet, luminous presence within every human soul. *The Over-Soul* is his attempt to name this presence and to describe how it manifests in thought, love, character, and creation.

Central to Emerson's argument is the conviction that each person contains a divine essence—a self that is deeper than personality, beyond the senses, and prior to social identity. This self, he contends, is not private or separate; it is a manifestation of a larger spiritual reality: the Over-Soul. It is at once immanent and transcendent, within and beyond, personal and universal. "We live in succession, in division, in parts, in particles," he writes. "Meantime within man is the soul of the whole; the wise silence; the universal beauty, to which every part and particle is equally related; the eternal ONE." This is the philosophical and poetic heart of the essay.

Emerson's prose here is deliberately enigmatic and elevated. He does not offer systematic arguments or theological proof. Instead, he unfolds a vision—slowly, elliptically, intuitively—using metaphor, paradox, and rhythmic insight to draw the reader into a deeper state of awareness. The result is not only a masterpiece of American spiritual literature but a gateway into an altered mode of consciousness: a way of seeing the world and the self with new reverence, clarity, and wholeness.

In this introduction, we will explore *The Over-Soul* as Emerson's definitive statement on the spiritual nature of human existence. We will examine the philosophical roots of the concept, its implications for ethics, art, love, and immortality, and its resonance with traditions as diverse as Vedanta, Neoplatonism, Quakerism, and Romantic idealism. We will also consider its relevance in our contemporary moment, where the search for deeper meaning, interconnection, and moral clarity remains as urgent as ever.

Emerson does not seek to persuade in the conventional sense; he seeks to awaken. He writes for the "inward eye"—for those who, amid the distractions of the world, still long to hear the "wise silence" within. As you begin reading *The Over-Soul*, do so with more than your intellect. Read with your heart, your intuition, and your whole being. Emerson's goal is not to give you answers, but to guide you toward the source from which all true answers arise.

Unity, Intuition, and Inner Revelation

To understand Emerson's vision in *The Over-Soul*, one must begin with his radical redefinition of selfhood. For Emerson, the "soul" is not merely the psychological interior of the individual—it is a point of access to the infinite. The true self, he insists, is not confined to thought or sensation. It is not the ego or the sum of life experiences. Rather, it is a "ray of relation to the eternal." What we typically think of as "I" is but the surface; beneath it lies a universal essence that is shared by all beings, beyond words, concepts, and personality.

Emerson is drawing here on a lineage of mystical and metaphysical traditions that describe the unity of all life. From the Vedantic idea of the Atman as the inner self identical with Brahman, to the Neoplatonic concept of the One from which all things emanate, Emerson synthesizes these insights into a uniquely American transcendental vocabulary. The Over-Soul is not an object of faith but an experience of presence. It is known not through external proof, but through *intuition*—a direct, unmediated knowing that arises when the mind is quiet, the ego recedes, and the "wise silence" speaks.

This intuition is the central epistemology of the Over-Soul. Unlike empirical knowledge, which depends on observation and logic, intuitive knowledge arises from within and reveals universal truths. "Whenever the mind is simple," Emerson writes, "and receives a divine wisdom, old things pass away,—means, teachers, texts, temples fall; it lives now, and absorbs past and future into the present hour." The authority of the soul is immediate and total. It needs no external sanction.

From this flows Emerson's sharp critique of religious formalism. He respects the ethical insights of religious traditions but warns against mistaking the form for the spirit. Scriptures, rituals, and institutions are only valid to the extent that they point inward—to the living presence of the Over-Soul in each heart. "The soul knows no persons," he writes, "proclaims no individuals. It is one." Thus, the divine is not a remote king enthroned in heaven, but an ever-present reality pulsing through all life.

The ethical implications of this idea are immense. If all people share the same spiritual essence, then justice, compassion, and equality are not optional—they are ontological imperatives. Love becomes the highest expression of spiritual realization—not romantic love alone, but agape: the recognition of the divine in the other. "All goes to show," Emerson writes, "that the soul in man is not an organ, but animates and exercises all the organs; is not a function, like the power of memory, of calculation, of comparison,—but uses these as hands and feet; is not a faculty, but a light."

To live in accord with the Over-Soul is to live from this light. It is to become, not a creature of circumstance, but an embodiment of eternal truth. It is to recognize that the same force that animates the star, the tree, and the child also animates you. And it is to realize that your highest dignity lies in aligning your life—your thought, your work, your relationships—with this silent, radiant presence.

Emerson's Mysticism and Modern Resonance

Perhaps the most profound and moving sections of *The Over-Soul* are those that touch on death, immortality, and the continuity of spirit. Emerson refuses to view death as annihilation. Instead, he sees it as a transition, a transformation of form, not essence. Because the Over-Soul is infinite and eternal, the individual soul—which is but a manifestation of the One—cannot be destroyed. "We are immortal with the immortality of the Soul," he writes. Death, in this view, is not a rupture, but a return.

This conviction arises not from dogma but from deep inner experience. Emerson speaks as one who has stood in the stillness and heard the echo of eternity. "I feel that nothing can befall me in life,—no disgrace, no calamity... which nature cannot repair." His faith is not in a future paradise, but in the sanctity and sufficiency of the present. The soul, rightly attuned, already dwells in eternity. "Time and space are but inverse measures of the force of the soul," he asserts. "The spirit sports with time."

This mystical sensibility, while shaped by the contemplative traditions of the East and the philosophical idealism of the West, is also deeply rooted in Emerson's own poetic temperament. He was not merely a philosopher, but a seer. His language carries the cadences of revelation, not argument. He does not seek to define the Over-Soul, but to gesture toward it, to evoke it, to name what cannot be named.

In our contemporary age—marked by fragmentation, secular anxiety, and ecological crisis—*The Over-Soul* offers a vision of radical interconnection and spiritual depth. Its message is not to escape the world but to see it anew: as sacred, as unified, as expressive of a deeper intelligence. In the face of environmental degradation, it calls us to recognize the divine in the earth. In the face of social injustice, it calls us to see the same spirit in every person. In the face of despair, it calls us inward—toward the still center where wisdom resides.

The challenge, of course, is to live from this awareness. Emerson never promises that the path is easy. The distractions of society, the illusions of ego, the inertia of habit—all conspire to dim the light of the soul. But the invitation remains. "Live ever in a new day," he writes. "Trust the soul." These are not quaint sentiments. They are commands of the spirit.

As you read *The Over-Soul*, let its rhythms draw you into stillness. Let its paradoxes disturb your assumptions. Let its vision enlarge your sense of self. This is not an essay to be analyzed alone—it is one to be experienced, to be read aloud, to be meditated upon. Emerson did not write it to impress, but to awaken. Not to instruct, but to inspire.

And if you find, as Emerson hoped, that something in you stirs in recognition—that a truth long known but long buried begins to flicker—then let that be the beginning. For you are not merely a reader. You are a soul. And the Over-Soul, vast and luminous, is speaking still

The Over-Soul

"But souls that of his own good life partake,
He loves as his own self; dear as his eye
They are to Him: He'll never them forsake:
When they shall die, then God himself shall die:
They live, they live in blest eternity."

Henry More.

Space is ample, east and west,
But two cannot go abreast,
Cannot travel in it two:
Yonder masterful cuckoo
Crowds every egg out of the nest,
Quick or dead, except its own;
A spell is laid on sod and stone,
Night and Day 've been tampered with,
Every quality and pith
Surcharged and sultry with a power
That works its will on age and hour.

There is a difference between one and another hour of life in their authority and subsequent effect. Our faith comes in moments; our vice is habitual. Yet there is a depth in those brief moments which constrains us to ascribe more reality to them than to all other experiences. For this reason the argument which is always forthcoming to silence those who conceive extraordinary hopes of man, namely the appeal to experience, is for ever invalid and vain. We give up the past to the objector, and yet we hope. He must explain this hope. We grant that human life is mean, but how did we find out that it was mean? What is the ground of this uneasiness of ours; of this old discontent? What is the universal sense of want and ignorance, but the fine innuendo by which the soul makes its enormous claim? Why do men feel that the natural history of man has never been written, but he is always leaving behind what you have said of him, and it becomes old, and books of metaphysics worthless? The philosophy of six thousand years has not searched the chambers and magazines of the soul. In its experiments there has always remained, in the last analysis, a residuum it could not resolve. Man is a stream whose source is hidden. Our being is descending into us from we know not whence. The most exact calculator has no prescience that somewhat incalculable may not balk the very next moment. I am constrained every moment to acknowledge a higher origin for events than the will I call mine.

As with events, so is it with thoughts. When I watch that flowing river, which, out of regions I see not, pours for a season its streams into me, I see that I am a pensioner; not a cause, but a surprised spectator of this ethereal water; that I desire and look up and put myself in the attitude of reception, but from some alien energy the visions come.

The Supreme Critic on the errors of the past and the present, and the only prophet of that which must be, is that great nature in which we rest as the earth lies in the soft arms of the atmosphere; that Unity, that Over-soul, within which every man's particular being is contained and made one with all other; that common heart of which all sincere conversation is the worship, to which all right action is submission; that overpowering reality which confutes our tricks and talents, and constrains every one to pass for what he is, and to speak from his character and not from his tongue, and which evermore tends to pass into our thought and hand and become wisdom and virtue and power and beauty. We live in succession, in division, in parts, in particles. Meantime within man is the soul of the whole; the wise silence; the universal beauty, to which every part and particle is equally related; the eternal ONE. And this deep power in which we exist and whose beatitude is all accessible to us, is not only self-sufficing and perfect in every hour, but the act of seeing and the thing seen, the seer and the spectacle, the subject and the object, are one. We see the world piece by piece, as the sun, the moon, the animal, the tree; but the whole, of which these are the shining parts, is the soul. Only by the vision of that Wisdom can the horoscope of the ages be read, and by falling back on our better thoughts, by yielding to the spirit of prophecy which is innate in every man, we can know what it saith. Every man's words who speaks from that life must sound vain to those who do not dwell in the same thought on their own part. I dare not speak for it. My words do not carry its august sense; they fall short and cold. Only itself can inspire whom it will, and behold! their speech shall be lyrical, and sweet, and universal as the rising of the wind. Yet I desire, even by profane words, if I may not use sacred, to indicate the heaven of this deity and to report what hints I have collected of the transcendent simplicity and energy of the Highest Law.

If we consider what happens in conversation, in reveries, in remorse, in times of passion, in surprises, in the instructions of dreams, wherein often we see ourselves in masquerade,—the droll disguises only magnifying and enhancing a real element and forcing it on our distinct notice,—we shall catch many hints that will broaden and lighten into knowledge of the secret of nature. All goes to show that the soul in man is not an organ, but animates and exercises all the organs; is not a function, like the power of memory, of calculation, of comparison, but uses these as hands and feet; is not a faculty, but a light; is not the intellect or the will, but the master of the intellect and the will; is the background of our being, in which they lie,—an immensity not possessed and that cannot be possessed. From within or from behind, a light shines through us upon things and makes us aware that we are nothing, but the light is all. A man is the facade of a temple wherein all wisdom and all good abide. What we commonly call man, the eating, drinking, planting, counting man, does not, as we know him, represent himself, but misrepresents himself. Him we do not respect, but the soul, whose organ he is, would he let it appear through his action, would make our knees bend. When it breathes through his intellect, it is genius; when it breathes through his will, it is virtue; when it flows through his affection, it is love. And the blindness of the intellect begins when it would be something of itself. The weakness of the will begins when the individual would be something of himself. All reform aims in some one particular to let the soul have its way through us; in other words, to engage us to obey.

Of this pure nature every man is at some time sensible. Language cannot paint it with his colors. It is too subtile. It is undefinable, unmeasurable; but we know that it pervades and contains us. We know that all spiritual being is in man. A wise old proverb says, "God comes to see us without bell;" that is, as there is no screen or ceiling between our heads and the infinite heavens, so is there no bar or wall in the soul where man, the effect, ceases, and God, the cause, begins. The walls are taken away. We lie open on one side to the deeps of spiritual nature, to the attributes of God. Justice we see and know, Love, Freedom, Power. These natures no man ever got above, but they tower over us, and most in the moment when our interests tempt us to wound them.

The sovereignty of this nature whereof we speak is made known by its independency of those limitations which circumscribe us on every hand. The soul circumscribes all things. As I have said, it contradicts all experience. In like manner it abolishes time and space. The influence of the senses has in most men overpowered the mind to that degree that the walls of time and space have come to look real and insurmountable; and to speak with levity of these limits is, in the world, the sign of insanity. Yet time and space are but inverse measures of the force of the soul. The spirit sports with time,—

"Can crowd eternity into an hour,
Or stretch an hour to eternity."

We are often made to feel that there is another youth and age than that which is measured from the year of our natural birth. Some thoughts always find us young, and keep us so. Such a thought is the love of the universal and eternal beauty. Every man parts from that contemplation with the feeling that it rather belongs to ages than to mortal life. The least activity of the intellectual powers redeems us in a degree from the conditions of time. In sickness, in languor, give us a strain of poetry or a profound sentence, and we are refreshed; or produce a volume of Plato or Shakspeare, or remind us of their names, and instantly we come into a feeling of longevity. See how the deep divine thought reduces centuries and millenniums and makes itself present through all ages. Is the teaching of Christ less effective now than it was when first his mouth was opened? The emphasis of facts and persons in my thought has nothing to do with time. And so always the soul's scale is one, the scale of the senses and the understanding is another. Before the revelations of the soul, Time, Space and Nature shrink away. In common speech we refer all things to time, as we habitually refer the immensely sundered stars to one concave sphere. And so we say that the Judgment is distant or near, that the Millennium approaches, that a day of certain political, moral, social reforms is at hand, and the like, when we mean that in the nature of things one of the facts we contemplate is external and fugitive, and the other is permanent and connate with the soul. The things we now esteem fixed shall, one by one, detach themselves like ripe fruit from our experience, and fall. The wind shall blow them none knows whither. The landscape, the figures, Boston, London, are facts as fugitive as any institution past, or any whiff of mist or smoke, and so is society, and so is the world. The soul looketh steadily forwards, creating a world before her, leaving worlds behind her. She has no dates, nor rites, nor persons, nor specialties nor men. The soul knows only the soul; the web of events is the flowing robe in which she is clothed.

After its own law and not by arithmetic is the rate of its progress to be computed. The soul's advances are not made by gradation, such as can be represented by motion in a straight line, but rather by ascension of state, such as can be represented by metamorphosis,—from the egg to the worm, from the worm to the fly. The growths of genius are of a certain total character, that does not advance the elect individual first over John, then Adam, then Richard, and give to each the pain of discovered inferiority,—but by every throe of growth the man expands there where he works, passing, at each pulsation, classes, populations, of men. With each divine impulse the mind rends the thin rinds of the visible and finite, and comes out into eternity, and inspires and expires its air. It converses with truths that have always been spoken in the world, and becomes conscious of a closer sympathy with Zeno and Arrian than with persons in the house.

This is the law of moral and of mental gain. The simple rise as by specific levity not into a particular virtue, but into the region of all the virtues. They are in the spirit which contains them all. The soul requires purity, but purity is not it; requires justice, but justice is not that; requires beneficence, but is somewhat better; so that there is a kind of descent and accommodation felt when we leave speaking of moral nature to urge a virtue which it enjoins. To the well-born child all the virtues are natural, and not painfully acquired. Speak to his heart, and the man becomes suddenly virtuous.

Within the same sentiment is the germ of intellectual growth, which obeys the same law. Those who are capable of humility, of justice, of love, of aspiration, stand already on a platform that commands the sciences and arts, speech and poetry, action and grace. For whoso dwells in this moral beatitude already anticipates those special powers which men prize so highly. The lover has no talent, no skill, which passes for quite nothing with his enamoured maiden, however little she may possess of related faculty; and the heart which abandons itself to the Supreme Mind finds itself related to all its works, and will travel a royal road to particular knowledges and powers. In ascending to this primary and aboriginal sentiment we have come from our remote station on the circumference instantaneously to the centre of the world, where, as in the closet of God, we see causes, and anticipate the universe, which is but a slow effect.

One mode of the divine teaching is the incarnation of the spirit in a form,—in forms, like my own. I live in society, with persons who answer to thoughts in my own mind, or express a certain obedience to the great instincts to which I live. I see its presence to them. I am certified of a common nature; and these other souls, these separated selves, draw me as nothing else can. They stir in me the new emotions we call passion; of love, hatred, fear, admiration, pity; thence come conversation, competition, persuasion, cities and war. Persons are supplementary to the primary teaching of the soul. In youth we are mad for persons. Childhood and youth see all the world in them. But the larger experience of man discovers the identical nature appearing through them all. Persons themselves acquaint us with the impersonal. In all conversation between two persons tacit reference is made, as to a third party, to a common nature. That third party or common nature is not social; it is impersonal; is God. And so in groups where debate is earnest, and especially on high questions, the company become aware that the thought rises to an equal level in all bosoms, that all have a spiritual property in what was said, as well as the sayer. They all become wiser than they were. It arches over them like a temple, this unity of thought in which every heart beats with nobler sense of power and duty, and thinks and acts with unusual solemnity. All are conscious of attaining to a higher self-possession. It shines for all. There is a certain wisdom of humanity which is common to the greatest men with the lowest, and which our ordinary education often labors to silence and obstruct. The mind is one, and the best minds, who love truth for its own sake, think much less of property in truth. They accept it thankfully everywhere, and do not label or stamp it with any man's name, for it is theirs long beforehand, and from eternity. The learned and the studious of thought have no monopoly of wisdom. Their violence of direction in some degree disqualifies them to think truly. We owe many valuable observations to people who are not very acute or profound, and who say the thing without effort which we want and have long been hunting in vain. The action of the soul is oftener in that which is felt and left unsaid than in that which is said in any conversation. It broods over every society, and they unconsciously seek for it in each other. We know better than we do. We do not yet possess ourselves, and we know at the same time that we are much more. I feel the same truth how often in my trivial conversation with my neighbors, that somewhat higher in each of us overlooks this by-play, and Jove nods to Jove from behind each of us.

Men descend to meet. In their habitual and mean service to the world, for which they forsake their native nobleness, they resemble those Arabian sheiks who dwell in mean houses and affect an external poverty, to escape the rapacity of the Pacha, and reserve all their display of wealth for their interior and guarded retirements.

As it is present in all persons, so it is in every period of life. It is adult already in the infant man. In my dealing with my child, my Latin and Greek, my accomplishments and my money stead me nothing; but as much soul as I have avails. If I am wilful, he sets his will against mine, one for one, and leaves me, if I please, the degradation of beating him by my superiority of strength. But if I renounce my will and act for the soul, setting that up as umpire between us two, out of his young eyes looks the same soul; he reveres and loves with me.

The soul is the perceiver and revealer of truth. We know truth when we see it, let skeptic and scoffer say what they choose. Foolish people ask you, when you have spoken what they do not wish to hear, 'How do you know it is truth, and not an error of your own?' We know truth when we see it, from opinion, as we know when we are awake that we are awake. It was a grand sentence of Emanuel Swedenborg, which would alone indicate the greatness of that man's perception,—"It is no proof of a man's understanding to be able to confirm whatever he pleases; but to be able to discern that what is true is true, and that what is false is false,—this is the mark and character of intelligence." In the book I read, the good thought returns to me, as every truth will, the image of the whole soul. To the bad thought which I find in it, the same soul becomes a discerning, separating sword, and lops it away. We are wiser than we know. If we will not interfere with our thought, but will act entirely, or see how the thing stands in God, we know the particular thing, and every thing, and every man. For the Maker of all things and all persons stands behind us and casts his dread omniscience through us over things.

But beyond this recognition of its own in particular passages of the individual's experience, it also reveals truth. And here we should seek to reinforce ourselves by its very presence, and to speak with a worthier, loftier strain of that advent. For the soul's communication of truth is the highest event in nature, since it then does not give somewhat from itself, but it gives itself, or passes into and becomes that man whom it enlightens; or, in proportion to that truth he receives, it takes him to itself.

We distinguish the announcements of the soul, its manifestations of its own nature, by the term Revelation. These are always attended by the emotion of the sublime. For this communication is an influx of the Divine mind into our mind. It is an ebb of the individual rivulet before the flowing surges of the sea of life. Every distinct apprehension of this central commandment agitates men with awe and delight. A thrill passes through all men at the reception of new truth, or at the performance of a great action, which comes out of the heart of nature. In these communications the power to see is not separated from the will to do, but the insight proceeds from obedience, and the obedience proceeds from a joyful perception. Every moment when the individual feels himself invaded by it is memorable. By the necessity of our constitution a certain enthusiasm attends the individual's consciousness of that divine presence. The character and duration of this enthusiasm varies with the state of the individual, from an ecstasy and trance and prophetic inspiration,—which is its rarer appearance,—to the faintest glow of virtuous emotion, in which form it warms, like our household fires, all the families and associations of men, and makes society possible. A certain tendency to insanity has always attended the opening of the religious sense in men, as if they had been "blasted with excess of light." The trances of Socrates, the "union" of Plotinus, the vision of Porphyry, the conversion of Paul, the aurora of Behmen, the convulsions of George Fox and his Quakers, the illumination of Swedenborg, are of this kind. What was in the case of these remarkable persons a ravishment, has, in innumerable instances in common life, been exhibited in less striking manner. Everywhere the history of religion betrays a tendency to enthusiasm. The rapture of the Moravian and Quietist; the opening of the internal sense of the Word, in the language of the New Jerusalem Church; the revival of the Calvinistic churches; the experiences of the Methodists, are varying forms of that shudder of awe and delight with which the individual soul always mingles with the universal soul.

The nature of these revelations is the same; they are perceptions of the absolute law. They are solutions of the soul's own questions. They do not answer the questions which the understanding asks. The soul answers never by words, but by the thing itself that is inquired after.

Revelation is the disclosure of the soul. The popular notion of a revelation is that it is a telling of fortunes. In past oracles of the soul the understanding seeks to find answers to sensual questions, and undertakes to tell from God how long men shall exist, what their hands shall do and who shall be their company, adding names and dates and places. But we must pick no locks. We must check this low curiosity. An answer in words is delusive; it is really no answer to the questions you ask. Do not require a description of the countries towards which you sail. The description does not describe them to you, and to-morrow you arrive there and know them by inhabiting them. Men ask concerning the immortality of the soul, the employments of heaven, the state of the sinner, and so forth. They even dream that Jesus has left replies to precisely these interrogatories. Never a moment did that sublime spirit speak in their patois. To truth, justice, love, the attributes of the soul, the idea of immutableness is essentially associated. Jesus, living in these moral sentiments, heedless of sensual fortunes, heeding only the manifestations of these, never made the separation of the idea of duration from the essence of these attributes, nor uttered a syllable concerning the duration of the soul. It was left to his disciples to sever duration from the moral elements, and to teach the immortality of the soul as a doctrine, and maintain it by evidences. The moment the doctrine of the immortality is separately taught, man is already fallen. In the flowing of love, in the adoration of humility, there is no question of continuance. No inspired man ever asks this question or condescends to these evidences. For the soul is true to itself, and the man in whom it is shed abroad cannot wander from the present, which is infinite, to a future which would be finite.

These questions which we lust to ask about the future are a confession of sin. God has no answer for them. No answer in words can reply to a question of things. It is not in an arbitrary "decree of God," but in the nature of man, that a veil shuts down on the facts of to-morrow; for the soul will not have us read any other cipher than that of cause and effect. By this veil which curtains events it instructs the children of men to live in to-day. The only mode of obtaining an answer to these questions of the senses is to forego all low curiosity, and, accepting the tide of being which floats us into the secret of nature, work and live, work and live, and all unawares the advancing soul has built and forged for itself a new condition, and the question and the answer are one.

By the same fire, vital, consecrating, celestial, which burns until it shall dissolve all things into the waves and surges of an ocean of light, we see and know each other, and what spirit each is of. Who can tell the grounds of his knowledge of the character of the several individuals in his circle of friends? No man. Yet their acts and words do not disappoint him. In that man, though he knew no ill of him, he put no trust. In that other, though they had seldom met, authentic signs had yet passed, to signify that he might be trusted as one who had an interest in his own character. We know each other very well,—which of us has been just to himself and whether that which we teach or behold is only an aspiration or is our honest effort also.

We are all discerners of spirits. That diagnosis lies aloft in our life or unconscious power. The intercourse of society, its trade, its religion, its friendships, its quarrels, is one wide, judicial investigation of character. In full court, or in small committee, or confronted face to face, accuser and accused, men offer themselves to be judged. Against their will they exhibit those decisive trifles by which character is read. But who judges? and what? Not our understanding. We do not read them by learning or craft. No; the wisdom of the wise man consists herein, that he does not judge them; he lets them judge themselves and merely reads and records their own verdict.

By virtue of this inevitable nature, private will is overpowered, and, maugre our efforts or our imperfections, your genius will speak from you, and mine from me. That which we are, we shall teach, not voluntarily but involuntarily. Thoughts come into our minds by avenues which we never left open, and thoughts go out of our minds through avenues which we never voluntarily opened. Character teaches over our head. The infallible index of true progress is found in the tone the man takes. Neither his age, nor his breeding, nor company, nor books, nor actions, nor talents, nor all together can hinder him from being deferential to a higher spirit than his own. If he have not found his home in God, his manners, his forms of speech, the turn of his sentences, the build, shall I say, of all his opinions will involuntarily confess it, let him brave it out how he will. If he have found his centre, the Deity will shine through him, through all the disguises of ignorance, of ungenial temperament, of unfavorable circumstance. The tone of seeking is one, and the tone of having is another.

The great distinction between teachers sacred or literary,—between poets like Herbert, and poets like

Pope,—between philosophers like Spinoza, Kant and Coleridge, and philosophers like Locke, Paley, Mackintosh and Stewart,—between men of the world who are reckoned accomplished talkers, and here and there a fervent mystic, prophesying half insane under the infinitude of his thought,—is that one class speak from within, or from experience, as parties and possessors of the fact; and the other class from without, as spectators merely, or perhaps as acquainted with the fact on the evidence of third persons. It is of no use to preach to me from without. I can do that too easily myself. Jesus speaks always from within, and in a degree that transcends all others. In that is the miracle. I believe beforehand that it ought so to be. All men stand continually in the expectation of the appearance of such a teacher. But if a man do not speak from within the veil, where the word is one with that it tells of, let him lowly confess it.

The same Omniscience flows into the intellect, and makes what we call genius. Much of the wisdom of the world is not wisdom, and the most illuminated class of men are no doubt superior to literary fame, and are not writers. Among the multitude of scholars and authors, we feel no hallowing presence; we are sensible of a knack and skill rather than of inspiration; they have a light and know not whence it comes and call it their own; their talent is some exaggerated faculty, some overgrown member, so that their strength is a disease. In these instances the intellectual gifts do not make the impression of virtue, but almost of vice; and we feel that a man's talents stand in the way of his advancement in truth. But genius is religious. It is a larger imbibing of the common heart. It is not anomalous, but more like and not less like other men. There is in all great poets a wisdom of humanity which is superior to any talents they exercise. The author, the wit, the partisan, the fine gentleman, does not take place of the man. Humanity shines in Homer, in Chaucer, in Spenser, in Shakspeare, in Milton. They are content with truth. They use the positive degree. They seem frigid and phlegmatic to those who have been spiced with the frantic passion and violent coloring of inferior but popular writers. For they are poets by the free course which they allow to the informing soul, which through their eyes beholds again and blesses the things which it hath made. The soul is superior to its knowledge, wiser than any of its works. The great poet makes us feel our own wealth, and then we think less of his compositions. His best communication to our mind is to teach us to despise all he has done. Shakspeare carries us to such a lofty strain of intelligent activity as to suggest a wealth which beggars his own; and we then feel that the splendid works which he has created, and which in other hours we extol as a sort of self-existent poetry, take no stronger hold of real nature than the shadow of a passing traveller on the rock. The inspiration which uttered itself in Hamlet and Lear could utter things as good from day to day for ever. Why then should I make account of Hamlet and Lear, as if we had not the soul from which they fell as syllables from the tongue?

This energy does not descend into individual life on any other condition than entire possession. It comes to the lowly and simple; it comes to whomsoever will put off what is foreign and proud; it comes as insight; it comes as serenity and grandeur. When we see those whom it inhabits, we are apprised of new degrees of greatness. From that inspiration the man comes back with a changed tone. He does not talk with men with an eye to their opinion. He tries them. It requires of us to be plain and true. The vain traveller attempts to embellish his life by quoting my lord and the prince and the countess, who thus said or did to him. The ambitious vulgar show you their spoons and brooches and rings, and preserve their cards and compliments. The more cultivated, in their account of their own experience, cull out the pleasing, poetic circumstance,—the visit to Rome, the man of genius they saw, the brilliant friend They know; still further on perhaps the gorgeous landscape, the mountain lights, the mountain thoughts they enjoyed yesterday,—and so seek to throw a romantic color over their life. But the soul that ascends to worship the great God is plain and true; has no rose-color, no fine friends, no chivalry, no adventures; does not want admiration; dwells in the hour that now is, in the earnest experience of the common day,—by reason of the present moment and the mere trifle having become porous to thought and bibulous of the sea of light.

Converse with a mind that is grandly simple, and literature looks like word-catching. The simplest utterances are worthiest to be written, yet are they so cheap and so things of course, that in the infinite riches of the soul it is like gathering a few pebbles off the ground, or bottling a little air in a phial, when the whole earth and the whole atmosphere are ours. Nothing can pass there, or make you one of the circle, but the casting aside your trappings, and dealing man to man in naked truth, plain confession, and omniscient affirmation.

Souls such as these treat you as gods would, walk as gods in the earth, accepting without any admiration your wit, your bounty, your virtue even,—say rather your act of duty, for your virtue they own as their proper blood, royal as themselves, and over-royal, and the father of the gods. But what rebuke their plain fraternal bearing casts on the mutual flattery with which authors solace each other and wound themselves! These flatter not. I do not wonder that these men go to see Cromwell and Christina and Charles the Second and James the First and the Grand Turk. For they are, in their own elevation, the fellows of kings, and must feel the servile tone of conversation in the world. They must always be a godsend to princes, for they confront them, a king to a king, without ducking or concession, and give a high nature the refreshment and satisfaction of resistance, of plain humanity, of even companionship and of new ideas. They leave them wiser and superior men. Souls like these make us feel that sincerity is more excellent than flattery. Deal so plainly with man and woman as to constrain the utmost sincerity and destroy all hope of trifling with you. It is the highest compliment you can pay. Their "highest praising," said Milton, "is not flattery, and their plainest advice is a kind of praising."

Ineffable is the union of man and God in every act of the soul. The simplest person who in his integrity worships God, becomes God; yet for ever and ever the influx of this better and universal self is new and unsearchable. It inspires awe and astonishment. How dear, how soothing to man, arises the idea of God, peopling the lonely place, effacing the scars of our mistakes and disappointments! When we have broken our god of tradition and ceased from our god of rhetoric, then may God fire the heart with his presence. It is the doubling of the heart itself, nay, the infinite enlargement of the heart with a power of growth to a new infinity on every side. It inspires in man an infallible trust. He has not the conviction, but the sight, that the best is the true, and may in that thought easily dismiss all particular uncertainties and fears, and adjourn to the sure revelation of time the solution of his private riddles. He is sure that his welfare is dear to the heart of being. In the presence of law to his mind he is overflowed with a reliance so universal that it sweeps away all cherished hopes and the most stable projects of mortal condition in its flood. He believes that he cannot escape from his good. The things that are really for thee gravitate to thee. You are running to seek your friend. Let your feet run, but your mind need not. If you do not find him, will you not acquiesce that it is best you should not find him? for there is a power, which, as it is in you, is in him also, and could therefore very well bring you together, if it were for the best. You are preparing with eagerness to go and render a service to which your talent and your taste invite you, the love of men and the hope of fame. Has it not occurred to you that you have no right to go, unless you are equally willing to be prevented from going? O, believe, as thou livest, that every sound that is spoken over the round world, which thou oughtest to hear, will vibrate on thine ear! Every proverb, every book, every byword that belongs to thee for aid or comfort, shall surely come home through open or winding passages. Every friend whom not thy fantastic will but the great and tender heart in thee craveth, shall lock thee in his embrace. And this because the heart in thee is the heart of all; not a valve, not a wall, not an intersection is there anywhere in nature, but one blood rolls uninterruptedly an endless circulation through all men, as the water of the globe is all one sea, and, truly seen, its tide is one.

Let man then learn the revelation of all nature and all thought to his heart; this, namely; that the Highest dwells with him; that the sources of nature are in his own mind, if the sentiment of duty is there. But if he would know what the great God speaketh, he must 'go into his closet and shut the door,' as Jesus said. God will not make himself manifest to cowards. He must greatly listen to himself, withdrawing himself from all the accents of other men's devotion. Even their prayers are hurtful to him, until he have made his own. Our religion vulgarly stands on numbers of believers. Whenever the appeal is made,—no matter how indirectly,—to numbers, proclamation is then and there made that religion is not. He that finds God a sweet enveloping thought to him never counts his company. When I sit in that presence, who shall dare to come in? When I rest in perfect humility, when I burn with pure love, what can Calvin or Swedenborg say?

It makes no difference whether the appeal is to numbers or to one. The faith that stands on authority is not faith. The reliance on authority measures the decline of religion, the withdrawal of the soul. The position men have given to Jesus, now for many centuries of history, is a position of authority. It characterizes themselves. It cannot alter the eternal facts. Great is the soul, and plain. It is no flatterer, it is no follower; it never appeals from itself. It believes in itself. Before the immense possibilities of man all mere experience, all past biography, however spotless and sainted, shrinks away. Before that heaven which our presentiments foreshow us, we cannot easily praise any form of life we have seen or read of. We not only affirm that we have few great men, but, absolutely speaking, that we have none; that we have no history, no record of any character or mode of living that entirely contents us. The saints and demigods whom history worships we are constrained to accept with a grain of allowance. Though in our lonely hours we draw a new strength out of their memory, yet, pressed on our attention, as they are by the thoughtless and customary, they fatigue and invade. The soul gives itself, alone, original and pure, to the Lonely, Original and Pure, who, on that condition, gladly inhabits, leads and speaks through it. Then is it glad, young and nimble. It is not wise, but it sees through all things. It is not called religious, but it is innocent. It calls the light its own, and feels that the grass grows and the stone falls by a law inferior to, and dependent on, its nature. Behold, it saith, I am born into the great, the universal mind. I, the imperfect, adore my own Perfect. I am somehow receptive of the great soul, and thereby I do Overlook the sun and the stars and feel them to be the fair accidents and effects which change and pass. More and more the surges of everlasting nature enter into me, and I become public and human in my regards and actions. So come I to live in thoughts and act with energies which are immortal. Thus revering the soul, and learning, as the ancient said, that "its beauty is immense," man will come to see that the world is the perennial miracle which the soul worketh, and be less astonished at particular wonders; he will learn that there is no profane history; that all history is sacred; that the universe is represented in an atom, in a moment of time. He will weave no longer a spotted life of shreds and patches, but he will live with a divine unity. He will cease from what is base and frivolous in his life and be content with all places and with any service he can render. He will calmly front the morrow in the negligency of that trust which carries God with it and so hath already the whole future in the bottom of the heart.

THE END

Thank You For Reading

You've Just Read a Piece of the Greatest Library Ever Rebuilt

Thank you for reading.

This book is one of thousands we're restoring, reimagining, and translating as part of the **Modern Library of Alexandria** — a global movement to preserve and share humanity's most important ideas.

What was once lost to fire and time is now rising again — not just as memory, but as living, breathing knowledge, freely accessible to all.

What You Can Do Next:

- **Keep Reading.**

  Discover more legendary works — in beautiful print, audiobook, or digital form — at LibraryofAlexandria.com.

- **Build Your Own Library.**

  Every title is available as a paperback, hardcover, or collectible boxset — at true printing cost. Craft a personal library worthy of display.

- **Spread the Light.**

  Share this book. Tell others about the movement. Help us translate every timeless work into every language, so no reader is ever left behind.

By finishing this book, you've already taken part in something extraordinary.

Join us at LibraryofAlexandria.com

Together, we're rebuilding the greatest library the world has ever known.

With appreciation,

The Modern Library of Alexandria Team

Visit:
www.libraryofalexandria.com
Or scan the code below:

www.ingramcontent.com/pod-product-compliance
Lightning Source LLC
Chambersburg PA
CBHW011453260626
47154CB00018B/3006
9781806681297